Wild Flowers

Hyacinth

Magnolia

Peony

Desert bluebell

Beaver-tail cactus

Buttercup

3

Common Flowers

Hibiscus

Sunflower

Champa

Mogra

Marigold

Gloxinia

Garden Perennials

Oleander

Zinnia

Dahlia

Chrysanthemum

Cosmos

Garden Perennials

Canna

Morning glory

Aster

Periwinkle

Pancy

Popular Flowers

Tulip

Rose

Gladiolus

Marigold

7

Balsam

Decorative Flowers

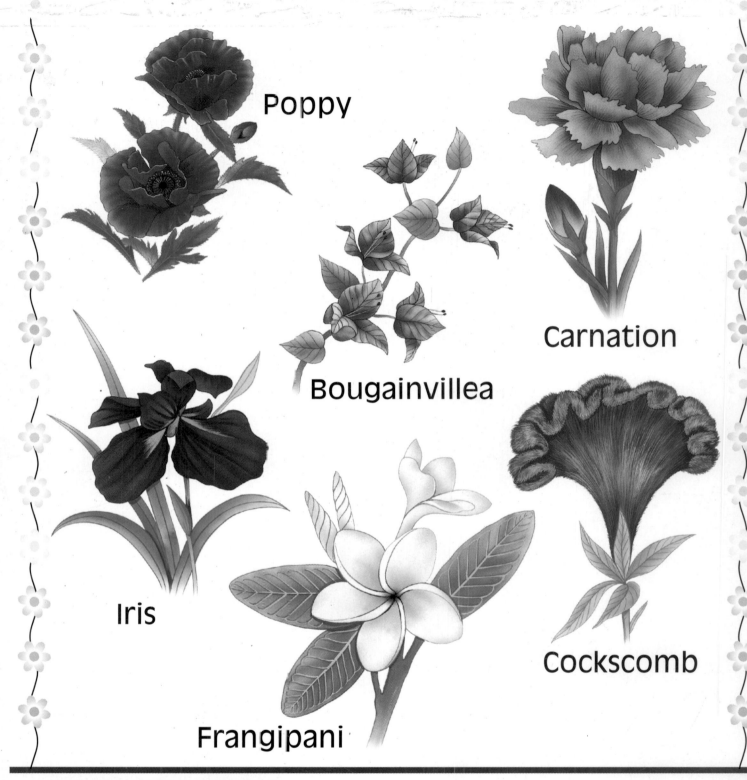

Poppy

Carnation

Bougainvillea

Iris

Frangipani

Cockscomb

MANOJ PUBLICATIONS

761, Main Road, Burari, Delhi-110084
Phones: 91-11-27611116, 27611349
Fax: 91-11-27611546 (**M**) 9868112194
E-mail : info@manojpublications.com
Website : www.manojpublications.com

Showroom :

1583-84, Dariba Kalan, Chandni Chowk, Delhi-110006
Phones : 91-11-23262174, 23268216 (**M**) 9818753569

CB-30

ISBN 81-310-0368-X

9 788131 003688

Price Rs. 25/-